DRAW the LINE

100+ Things You Can Do to CHANGE the WORLD!

Street Noise Books • Brooklyn, New York

ISBN 978-1951-491-15-4

Text by Myfanwy Tristram and Jeff Campbell

Edited by Jeff Campbell and Liz Frances
Draw the Line logo by Karrie Fransman
Additional front matter art by Woodrow Phoenix
Book design by Liz Frances

Printed in South Korea

9 8 7 6 5 4 3 2 1

First Edition

ACTION LIST!

1. ☐ Join the crowd.
2. ☐ Put a pin on it.
3. ☐ Shop local.
4. ☐ Go green in the bathroom.
5. ☐ **Be kind to others.**
6. ☐ Make an old-school zine.
7. ☐ **Be who you are.**
8. ☐ Don't fall for fake news.
9. ☐ **Lower the temperature.**
10. ☐ Share your message.
11. ☐ **Bee friendly.**
12. ☐ Use the power of laughter.
13. ☐ **Stand up to bullying.**
14. ☐ Layer up.
15. ☐ **Don't assume gender.**
16. ☐ Decorate your house.
17. ☐ **Be heard.**
18. ☐ Hang up a welcome sign.
19. ☐ **Eschew the new.**
20. ☐ Question the narrative.
21. ☐ **Share your experiences.**
22. ☐ Click it to fix it.
23. ☐ **Be supportive.**
24. ☐ Exert peer pressure.
25. ☐ **Raise a better generation.**
26. ☐ Have genuine conversations.
27. ☐ **See everyone.**
28. ☐ Diversify your bookshelf.
29. ☐ **Share your stuff.**
30. ☐ Raise funds.
31. ☐ **Get creative.**
32. ☐ Game the system.
33. ☐ **Refuse to shut up.**
34. ☐ Be political.
35. ☐ **Join the party.**
36. ☐ Plan, gather, protest.
37. ☐ **Reduce, reuse, recycle.**
38. ☐ Track your bills.

39 ☐ Give mindfully.

40 ☐ Write, publish, persuade.

41 ☐ Recognize oppression.

42 ☐ Feel better by helping others.

43 ☐ Become an events manager.

44 ☐ Start a petition.

45 ☐ Add a hashtag.

46 ☐ Spend wisely.

47 ☐ Become a big Twitter fish.

48 ☐ Vote, vote, vote.

49 ☐ Pop your bubble.

50 ☐ Face your nemesis.

51 ☐ Get off your arse.

52 ☐ Do your research.

53 ☐ Know your representatives.

54 ☐ Meme it up.

55 ☐ Put your money where your mouth is.

56 ☐ Organize a charity event.

57 ☐ Donate your castoffs.

58 ☐ Create community.

59 ☐ Watch your words.

60 ☐ Support a food drive.

61 ☐ Expand your kids' world.

62 ☐ Be a witness.

63 ☐ Plant a tree.

64 ☐ Amplify your voice.

65 ☐ Find your comfort zone.

66 ☐ Travel more slowly.

67 ☐ Invest in your community.

68 ☐ Listen with an open mind.

69 ☐ Reread history.

70 ☐ Eat less meat.

71 ☐ Create a barter economy.

72 ☐ Switch to green.

73 ☐ Help out refugees.

74 ☐ Crank up the Singer.

75 ☐ Question the new norms.

76 ☐ Buy clothes that last.

77 ☐ Send a letter of comfort.

78 ☐ Interpret a new life.

79 ☐ **Donate skills.**

80 ☐ Smile, don't stare.

81 ☐ **Promote a living wage.**

82 ☐ Write (and share) music.

83 ☐ **Tell stories.**

84 ☐ Broadcast your message.

85 ☐ **Call it out.**

86 ☐ Forage for dinner.

87 ☐ **Build a wall of kindness.**

88 ☐ Don't waste food.

89 ☐ **Take back the night.**

90 ☐ Don't take it on.

91 ☐ **Put your phone down.**

92 ☐ Remember the past.

93 ☐ **Listen to refugees.**

94 ☐ Meet the neighbors.

95 ☐ **Start a casserole club.**

96 ☐ Volunteer!

97 ☐ **Go large.**

98 ☐ Have your day in court.

99 ☐ **Be a Raging Granny.**

100 ☐ Run for office.

101 ☐ **Don't join the circus.**

102 ☐ Encourage someone's voice.

103 ☐ **Teach a language.**

104 ☐ Be a mentor.

105 ☐ **Plant radical roots.**

106 ☐ Stand up for immigrants.

107 ☐ **Rewire the grid.**

108 ☐ Become a community sponsor.

109 ☐ **Embrace craftivism.**

110 ☐ Hack your streets.

111 ☐ **Practice shop dropping.**

112 ☐ See people's potential.

113 ☐ **Leave water.**

114 ☐ Donate your art.

115 ☐ **Let enough be enough.**

116 ☐ Break the law.

This book presents more than 100 actions that anyone can take if they want to make a positive difference in the world. Some you can take right now; many can be done on the cheap or for no money at all; some are suitable for kids.

All of them have one thing in common: They encourage you to get involved. This book will inspire you to lend a hand and your voice to help tackle the issues you're most passionate about. There are suggestions for assisting those in need, improving the political climate, tackling social injustice and bias, fighting climate change, building supportive communities, and much more.

Why comics?

For most people, comic artist isn't the first occupation that comes to mind when they think about driving political change. After all, comics are supposed to be frivolous and fun and mostly for kids . . . aren't they? Of course, comics are fun, and many are for kids, but they certainly don't have to be frivolous. Not only does political cartooning have a long history, but today's fertile graphic novel and small-press scenes are also putting out an abundance of persuasive, thoughtful, political work for adults.

Comics can touch the soul like no other art form. They can tackle any subject, no matter how serious, with storytelling that combines memoir, reportage, and flights of fancy. Beautiful pieces of artwork in their own right—that is part of their power—comics are easy to access, quick to read . . . and then pow! They pack a punch. An ever-increasing wave of graphic novelists have aimed to use the form to untangle complex social, political, and personal realms.

Drawing the line.

Draw the Line started as a very modest project. Myfanwy Tristram envisioned bringing just five or six friends on board to make a small press comic, but the idea lit a spark. In a few days, it snowballed into the project you see today, with more than 100 artists keen to take part. They've illustrated some top tips for becoming politically engaged and changing the world— with more at drawthelinecomics.com/next-steps. Now it's your turn to get to it!

And please look out for the gavel icon throughout the book. You'll see it beside those ideas that may not be, hmm, shall we say strictly legal. If you are planning to take one of these actions, you do so at your own risk. We'd suggest you think it through and take extra care. And we take no responsibility for any loss or damage arising from your choices.

Nicholas Sputnik Miller

Join the crowd.

Signing a petition is so easy that it almost seems too easy. Can writing your name down really change anything? Yes, it can—particularly when you add your voice to a chorus of others asking for or supporting the same thing. Petitions are one mechanism for putting legislative initiatives on election ballots. Rules vary by nation and state, but petitions are often the first step for making new laws that improve our world.

And when you sign a petition, share it. If you feel moved and inspired, move and inspire others, too. Create a crowd that can't be ignored.

Sean Azzopardi

Put a pin on it.

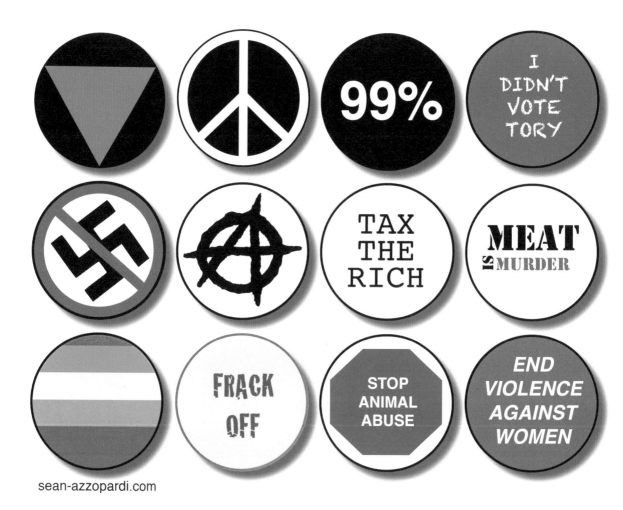

sean-azzopardi.com

Let the world know what you think without having to ask. Pins are tiny billboards that broadcast your message to everyone passing by. Political campaign buttons have been around since America's first presidential campaign, but today, handcrafted enamel pins are seriously fashion forward! Look good and speak loudly by wearing these tiny designer artworks.

Lucy Knisley

Shop local.

Political activism doesn't get more pleasant or enjoyable than shopping locally. Not only do you get to experience the warm glow of satisfaction that comes from directly supporting your community, but the people running those small businesses often become friends. When it's time to shop, take a walk and spend your money where you live.

Jo Harrison

Go green in the bathroom.

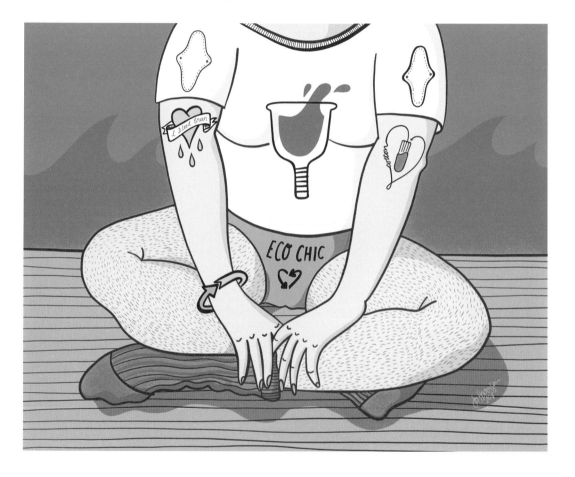

Bathrooms involve, well, a lot of waste—but that gives you lots of ways to go green. Like taking shorter showers; using biodegradable toothbrushes, dental floss, and cotton swabs; and using unbleached toilet paper made from recycled materials.

Here's an idea: Reusable sanitary products are a powerful way for menstruating people to minimize environmental impact (and save money). One estimate is that the average woman uses over 10,000 tampons in her lifetime! Menstrual cups and period panties are eco-friendly alternatives to the standard single-use disposable options.

Be kind to others.

WOODROW PHOENIX

Maybe it sounds trite, but showing kindness to others, especially to the disadvantaged, is one of the most powerful actions anyone can take. This starts with seeing people as people and recognizing our common humanity. A homeless person on the street is no different from any of us, and homelessness could happen to anyone.

That said, we don't need to know why someone is struggling, alone, hungry, or in pain to be kind. A simple gesture like a smile, a friendly word, or buying someone something to eat won't solve that person's problems, and it won't fix homelessness, but it will make that person's day brighter. Actually, two people. When we show compassion and help someone feel less alone, we feel less alone, too.

Rachael House

Make an old-school zine.

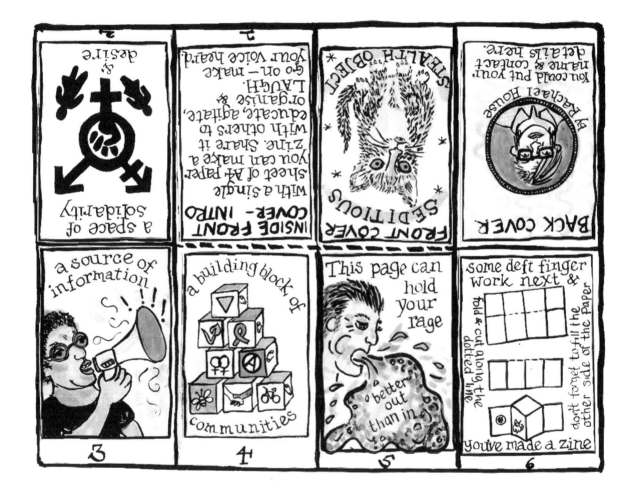

Want to party—and protest—like it's 1985 (or perhaps 1999)? Kick it old school and write, draw, cut, paste, and copy your very own self-published zine. These photocopied works of art, slapdash by design, are a great way to make your political point. Update and remix the original punk and riot grrrl aesthetic, and hand out your DIY masterpiece at the next gathering, gig, or march. Plus, if you want to boost circulation, you can also post it online.

Be who you are.

fig 1 ~ KNOW YOURSELF

Who am I?
Who am I?
Who am I?
Who am I?
KNOWN
UNEXPLORED
UNKNOWN
NOT YET INVENTED
UNDISCOVERED
UNIMAGINED
?
HIDDEN DEPTHS

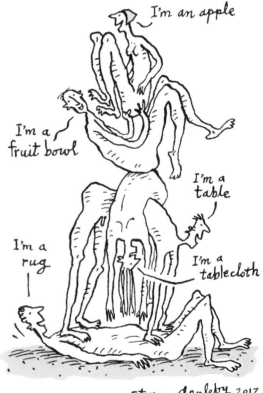

fig 2 ~ BE YOURSELF

I'm an apple
I'm a fruit bowl
I'm a table
I'm a rug
I'm a tablecloth

steven appleby 2017

Effective activism starts by knowing yourself, then being yourself. To help others in the best ways, it helps to know who you are. People aren't all the same, and we can't all help in the same ways. Explore what makes you tick, what brings you joy, your essential self, and then be who you are, unapologetically. And help others do the same.

Roger Langridge

Don't fall for fake news.

There's nothing new about "fake news," conspiracy theories, tabloid journalism, and clickbait. Just page through Britain's *The Sun* and *Daily Mail* and America's *National Enquirer.* Why do these tabloids even still exist? Because peddling falsehoods and sensationalism works! It sells papers, confuses the public about what's true, and can discredit the innocent and legitimate news sources. So before sharing that Facebook or Twitter post exposing the shocking, shocking corruption no one is reporting . . . do a little investigating of your own and make sure that news isn't totally, you know, fake.

Al Davison

Lower the temperature.

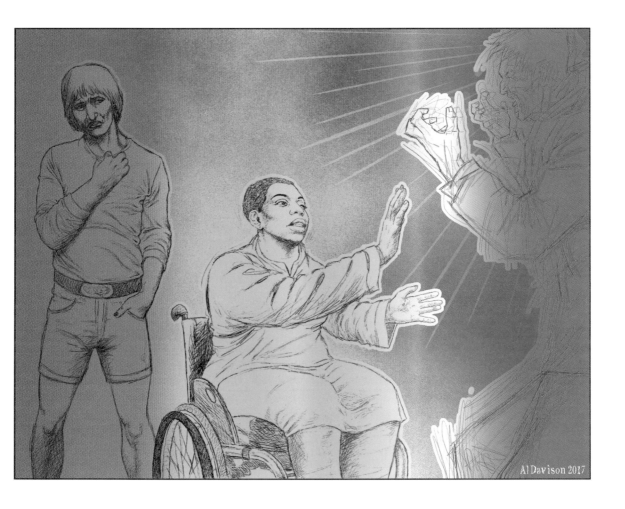

It's hard, if not impossible, to have reasonable discussions and solve problems if people become too angry and upset or too intimidated to speak. As much as possible, when conflicts arise—whether online or face-to-face, whether about politics or anything else—seek to lower the temperature by meeting outrage with calm.

Mijal Bloch

Share your message.

Mijal Bloch - Minsk

Whatever you believe in, share that message. When we put our ideas out into the world, we often find many others who share our perspective and concerns. Connecting with others who are already working for causes we feel strongly about is encouraging, and it can help us become more effective. Plus, the more people share the same message, the more people those calls to action will attract.

Bee friendly.

Declining bee populations are a worldwide crisis since about two-thirds of crop plants depend on pollination. In North America, about a quarter of the continent's 4,000 bee species are at risk of extinction, and half are in decline. Bees are struggling for four main reasons: loss of habitat, pesticides, disease, and climate change.

Anyone can help with the first two problems by creating pesticide-free, bee-friendly gardens and yards full of wildflowers. Contact Friends of the Earth for a "bee saver kit" to help keep our world buzzing.

Jim Medway

Use the power of laughter.

Humor is a recognized form of nonviolent protest, and it's available to anyone. You don't need to be a stand-up comedian to mock a dictator or skewer the sanctimonious. Sly wit and satire are in fact extremely persuasive—as political cartoonists have long known. Jokes win people over and can critique with devastating effectiveness.

Most of all? Whenever fear, anxiety, and panic threaten to take hold, nothing helps us feel better than having a good laugh.

Cesar Lador

Stand up to bullying.

If you see someone being bullied—online, at work, at school, at home, or in public—stand up for that person. Don't be a bystander. Most of all, get help to expose and confront the person who is bullying. This protects and supports the person being victimized, so they won't feel alone. It might even help change the mind or attitude of the other person.

Layer up.

If you want to save money while saving the planet, do what your mom always says: Turn the heat down—and layer up. In cold weather, knock back the thermostat, especially overnight. Wrap yourself in Grandma's knitted scarf, and add another blanket on the bed. Any strategy to use less energy helps the climate.

Siiri Viljakka

Don't assume gender.

Terms for gender identity and sexual orientation are changing dramatically—and it can be easy to feel left behind. But the new vocabulary reflects how language is catching up with all the diverse ways people experience identity, and it's wonderful that our dictionaries can expand to provide expression for all.

The most important thing, though, isn't learning new terms but asking others what they want to be called. Assumptions based on appearance won't always be correct, so let someone say if they identify as "she," "he," "they," or something else.

Decorate your house.

In Cardiff, Wales, a very cranky man once decorated the exterior of his home, top to bottom, with long written diatribes against the local city council. He was mad and wanted everyone to know why. For seventeen years, the "scream house," as people called it, became a unique form of outsider art that caught the attention of the world.

You, too, can use your house or window as a political billboard. You don't have to scream or protest. What do you want to say? Paint that message or just put up a poster and share your beliefs with delivery people, visitors, and passersby. In the place where you live, make clear where you stand.

Be heard.

If you see an urgent problem or something you want to change, speak out. Be heard. Shout. Don't be afraid to be as loud as you need to be to get people's attention. When the world is on fire, someone needs to yell, "Fire!"

Of course, no one likes a crank. Don't only scream. Once you've got someone's attention, practice the other advice in this book about treating others respectfully and having civil conversations. But sometimes, the only way to get attention in the first place is to stand up and let fly.

Sally-Anne Hickman

Hang up a welcome sign.

If your local or national government is making certain groups of people feel unwelcome or unsafe, declare the opposite in your home, workplace, or town. In 2016, when then-President Trump enacted a ban on Muslims and promised to build a border wall with Mexico, a printing cooperative in Portland, Oregon, created letterpress posters of welcome and made them available for free. The message was simple: "All are welcome here"; the idea was to hang them in your shop, office, or public space.

In our increasingly divided and divisive world, maybe the most important message is openness and inclusion. Hang up a welcome sign where you work and where you live, on your car, on your backpack, and on your Facebook page. Practice welcoming others of all persuasions, even when that's uncomfortable or difficult.

Eschew the new.

The backgrounds in this cartoon were all scanned from stuff bought in charity shops.

Buy secondhand. If it's new to you, isn't that new enough? In addition, if you buy from a thrift store, you'll be benefiting a charity, and if you buy direct from the seller, you'll be circumventing big business. Either way, buying used shrinks your carbon footprint.

Landis Blair

Question the narrative.

In our media-saturated world, it's important not to take everything we read or watch at face value. We can't be passive consumers. Be aware of who makes the news, and be alert for unconscious bias. This isn't about being cynical; it's about taking responsibility for our own media literacy.

After all, every story can be presented in a variety of ways, and no story can capture every perspective. Ask: What isn't being shown? And is what's shown accurate? Question the narrative, and teach your children to do the same. Then, call out inaccuracies and bias when you see them. That part's easy—just shout at your TV or radio.

Richy K. Chandler

Share your experiences.

As you cope with life's difficulties and try to improve the world, share your personal experiences. We can often feel isolated in our struggles, but expressing ourselves minimizes the pain. Further, we may find that others are feeling the same way. They can be uplifted to discover they aren't alone, and their appreciation of us can lift our spirits. Communication itself can be a radical, healing act.

Click it to fix it.

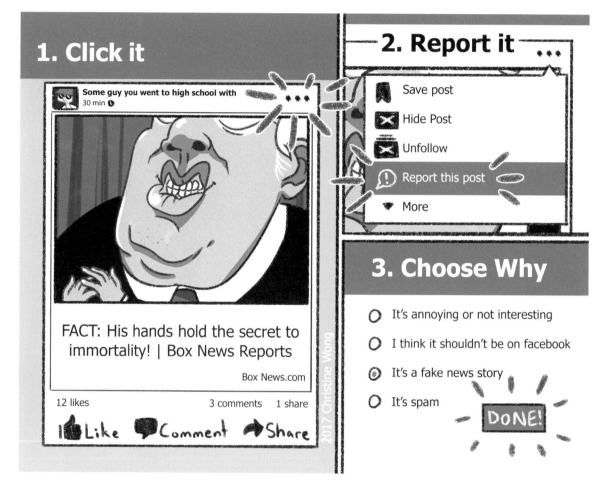

If you see an ad or post on social media that you don't like—because it spreads hate, lies, or misinformation, or is offensive and unwanted—report that post to the platform itself. On Facebook, three dots in the top-right corner lead to a hidden menu where you can block posts, unfollow users, and report problems. Most social media sites provide this function.

While blocking particular advertisers and users makes your personal social mediaverse more enjoyable, this has an aggregate effect, too. If advertisers receive lots of complaints, social media platforms might decide to restrict them or even block them entirely. After all, social media companies are businesses that have an interest in keeping their users happy.

Josie Pearse

Be supportive.

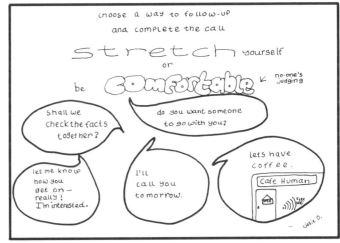

When current events and the political climate affect someone you know, perhaps in very specific ways—maybe because of their beliefs, race, sexuality, or lifestyle—reach out, see how they are doing, and be supportive. Do you know someone who may be feeling fear and anxiety because of current events right now? Let them know you've got their back. You'd be surprised how much good a few kind words can do.

H-P Lehkonen

Exert peer pressure.

Peer pressure is a remarkably powerful tool. It makes politics personal. If you feel that frequenting certain businesses or buying certain products supports unethical practices or causes, let your friends know. Of course, they might not agree, but they also might not realize the impact of their choices. Keep it up, and soon they'll be the ones reminding you!

Raise a better generation.

Kids are the voters of tomorrow. If you are a parent or teacher, make sure to impart solid values and a good understanding of the way the world works. Talk to them about unfairness in the world. Teach them equality and understanding. Help them understand their rights, and the rights of others. Let them know that our elected officials are available, and how to access them when we need them.

If you feel a political figure has let you down, tell your child about that, too. People are fallible, even those in power, and that's an important lesson to learn.

Rakel Stammer

Have genuine conversations.

Have conversations that help you understand the opposite points of view

Genuine conversation involves listening as much as explaining. Particularly when someone thinks differently, seek to understand their point of view rather than impose your own. When we talk with the goal to learn about and understand someone else, that makes for much more useful dialogues. In the end, even when people don't agree, sincere listening shows respect and helps heal any sense of division and conflict.

See everyone.

No matter what you do, and in every area of life, be aware of and see the incredible diversity that exists in the world. Account for all perspectives, anticipate all needs, and invite or include all people.

If you're an artist of any kind, remember to represent that diversity in your work. By showing people from marginalized communities and from various backgrounds, you can promote and normalize what a diverse society looks like.

Amanda Priebe

Diversify your bookshelf.

Who's on your bookshelf? What books do you read? Take a survey right now. Do most of the authors look like you? Are most books from the same genre? Whatever the case, seek to diversify the stories you read. Buy books by authors who represent cultures, ethnicities, and perspectives you know nothing about. It's a win-win: Not only will you increase your knowledge and expand your worldview, but you will help create a marketplace that supports diverse authors.

Share your stuff.

I'VE MADE GREAT USE OF OUR NEIGHBORHOOD SHARING SCHEME...

SAJ NEXT DOOR'S ROOF LADDERS

SIMON'S DEHUMIDIFIER

ANDY'S EXCELLENT SEWING MACHINE

HOWEVER, THE ITEMS I'VE BEEN OFFERING HAVE YET TO BE BORROWED...

MAGIC SET (INSTRUCTIONS MISSING)

SNOW GLOBES

VINTAGE YUGOSLAVIAN MATCH BOXES

JOE DECIE

Among friends and neighbors, create a sharing group for all those expensive tools and items—tall ladders, table saws, snowblowers, lawn mowers, canoes—that we all need sometimes, just not all the time. If every house on your street, or every apartment in your building, owned everything they might ever need, that would benefit only one thing—capitalism!

Sharing saves money and lessens the total amount of stuff in the world (thereby helping the environment) while also fostering community. And if sharing ladders goes well, think bigger, like sharing cars . . .

Steve Reynolds

Raise funds.

Now more than ever, charities and services need money. But even when money is tight, that doesn't mean we can't help. Get creative and make something useful or entertaining to sell on behalf of a charity. Do what you enjoy, whether that's gardening, drawing pictures, or performing. Best of all, it's a way to have fun while doing good.

Get creative.

Art speaks loudly, and you don't need to be Leonardo da Vinci to create it. Paint a picture, make a movie, write a song, decorate your home, knit a blanket, paste a collage, draw a comic, perform in public. Express yourself in your own way to touch the hearts, and minds, of others.

Game the system.

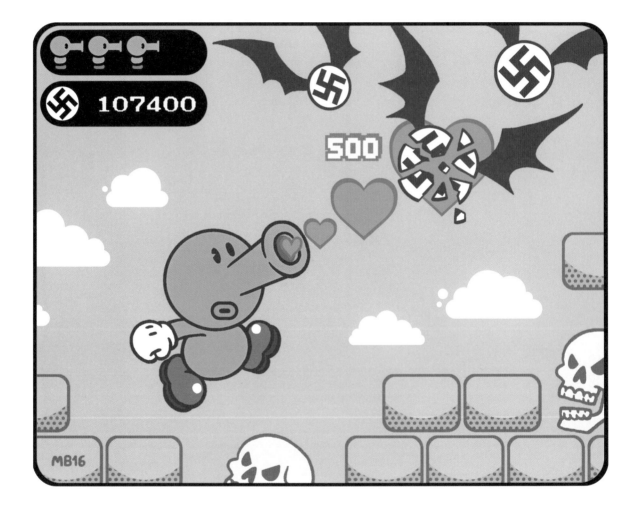

If you're a coder or a game designer, consider making online games and quizzes that promote a political message or that educate people about a complex issue. People love games and contests, so why not make education part of the competition? That way, players achieve more than just a high score.

Simon Russell

Refuse to shut up.

Tell your elected representative what you expect them to do about the issues that matter to you. And keep telling them. Even if you only receive a pat, generic response, don't shut up. Keep writing and communicating your expectations. We have to do more than vote. It's our job to hold our representatives accountable for the jobs they are doing.

Be political.

Get actively involved in politics. Everyone has political opinions, but politics itself is driven by those who show up. Attend local meetings for causes you care about—and you'll also create an instant, new social circle, filled with people who share your worldview, with the added bonus that, together, you might change the world.

Join the party.

To increase your influence, become a card-carrying member of your preferred political party, and join its local committee or organization. This way, you help support and shape the party itself, particularly on the local level, affecting where you live. You can vote on important party decisions and platforms, get to know the local leadership, and maybe even put yourself in position to become one of the organization's leaders yourself.

Simon Russell

Plan, gather, protest.

| | | | | | | | | | | | | | | | | | | | | | | | | | | | | | | | | |

FUME

LEARN

             PLAN

               ORGANISE

ACT

CHANGE

CHANGE

CHANGE

CHANGE

The Dissent of Man
(...and woman and child)

COMPLAIN
It's so easy to get angry at the state of the world today. But what can one person do?
A lone voice in the wilderness is easily ignored!

CONNECT
Social media lets you share your grievance with like-minded people, and research suitable locations and dates to take your message to the powers-that-be.

CONVENE
Fellow travellers can spread your ideas through their own network of contacts on social media – it is the perfect tool for growing awareness exponentially!

PROTEST
You can gather legally in public places to protest as a 'static assembly'. If there's no march organised as part of your protest, you don't have to tell the police about it.

MARCH
Processions are more heavily regulated but they are also (a bit) harder to ignore! Organisers must tell the police in writing the date/time/route of the march, plus the names and addresses of organisers 6 days before a public march.

inbrief.co.uk/human-rights/peaceful-protest

The evolution of a protest often starts with a single person whose anger becomes the catalyst for community solidarity. These days, thanks to social media, it's never been easier to share our feelings in public. But take your outrage offline as well, because it's also never been easier to organize, plan, and gather in the streets to demonstrate against injustice. Your feet were made for walking, so get marching.

36

Daniel Locke

Reduce, reuse, recycle.

We can each make a difference to improve the environment, reduce pollution, protect other species, and even fight climate change if we live by the mantra "Reduce, reuse, recycle." Seek to replace one-use, disposable items with permanent or reusable options. Convenience be hanged! Bring your own canvas tote bag to the grocery store and your own travel mug to the coffee shop. Mend torn clothes, repair a dinged bike, recycle plastic packaging, wear that coat another year. When it comes to waste, less is more.

Track your bills.

To protest effectively and make our voices count, we need to know when important legislation and bills are due for votes. Government websites post their legislative calendars online, and they are increasingly offering online notification services that provide updates on selected bills. If your state or national government does this, subscribe!

Then, when you know an important vote is coming up, contact your representative and tell them how you want them to vote—and get your friends to do the same. If politicians don't know how we feel, how can we expect them to represent us the way we want?

Dave McKean

Give mindfully.

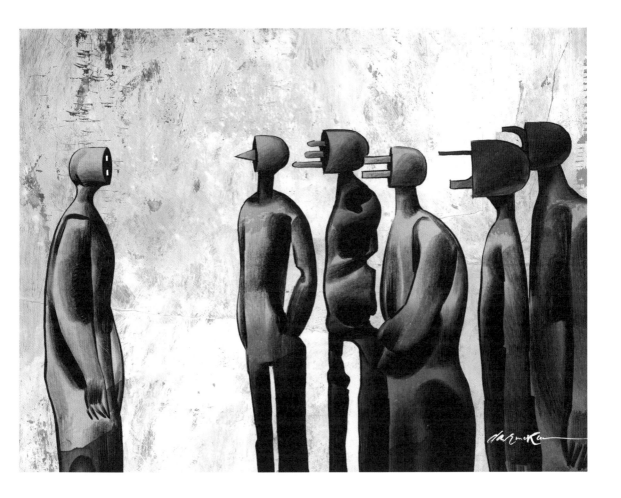

The world is full of worthy causes, but no single person can help everybody. So when you donate, donate mindfully. Connect to the cause or causes that share your values and inspire you the most. Then stay plugged in and support them in as many ways as you can. That will be more effective and feel more satisfying.

Keijjo Ahlqvist

Write, publish, persuade.

OUR PARENTS WROTE TO THE LETTERS PAGE OF THEIR LOCAL PRESS.

THESE DAYS, WITH ONLINE SPACE TO FILL, MANY PUBLICATIONS

ARE HAPPY TO ACCEPT HIGH-QUALITY THINK PIECES FROM THE PUBLIC.

FOR LOCAL ISSUES, APPROACH YOUR REGIONAL PRESS AND GET YOUR COMMUNITY ONSIDE.

FOR NATIONAL ISSUES, GO BIG. **START** WRITING.

AND THERE WILL BE OTHERS

Writing is often the best way to make your voice heard and to persuade others. Writing is also a great way to clarify and sharpen your thoughts so you can be more persuasive. If you are new to writing for a public readership, start small; respond to other articles via comments and letters to the editor as you hone your writing chops. If you feel comfortable writing, launch a regular blog or draft editorials and submit them to local, regional, and national publications. Once you put your thoughts out there, you never know who you will reach and influence.

Jeroen Janssen

Recognize oppression.

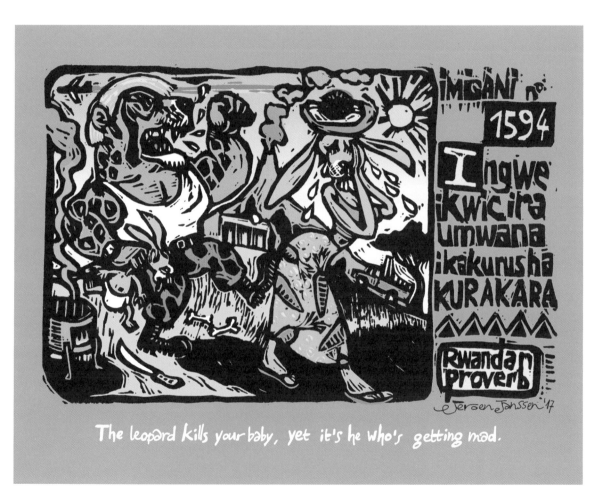

The leopard kills your baby, yet it's he who's getting mad.

When those in power blame the victims of abuse for their suffering, recognize this as a form of intimidation and oppression. When authority figures justify harmful actions by claiming that those who were hurt deserved it—and then they become angry when anyone contradicts them—recognize this as a self-serving rationale to maintain power. Call out hypocrisy when you see it.

Nate Macabuag

Feel better by helping others.

Feeling blah, run-down, and depressed about the state of our divided, troubled world? Don't just sit there, do something—for someone else! Research shows that volunteering in your community can actually raise your happiness levels. Or take a tip from His Holiness the Dalai Lama, who said, "If you want others to be happy, practice compassion. If you want to be happy, practice compassion."

Yen Quach

Become an events manager.

Don't wait around for someone else to organize community actions, protests, and political advocacy. When people need managing, be the one to do it. Getting started is as simple as making a checklist. Once you know what needs to be done, coordinate others and assign tasks. After all, most people are eager to pitch in; they just need someone to tell them what to do. That can be you!

Start a petition.

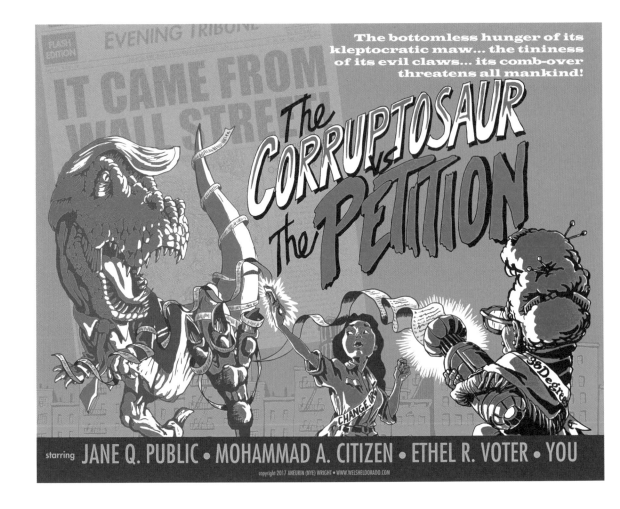

Don't just sign a petition. Create your own and gather support for the issues you care about. With a petition, citizens can directly challenge big business, politicians, and government institutions and create social change. The organization Change.org provides templates and advice to help coordinate campaigns around the globe, while 38 Degrees is a UK-based group doing much the same there.

Zoe N. Sugg

Add a hashtag.

Social media campaigns can be hugely effective in getting the word out to the masses, and memorable hashtags are the engines that drive them. Take inspiration from #Movember or #IceBucketChallenge and create a hashtag that gets attention and helps people show support, connect, and spread the word. Not sure what makes a great hashtag? Just keep it short and memorable, don't include spaces or punctuation, and you're #onyourway.

Spend wisely.

Read up on the stores and businesses where you shop: Do they pay their workers a living wage? Or do they support sweatshops or child labor? Do they fund the weapons industry or finance a political party that you disagree with?

Also investigate the products you buy: Are they cruelty-free, made without animal testing, and produced in sustainable and environmentally friendly ways? Support the companies and brands that reflect your ethics. Many apps and websites can help guide you.

Deborah Fajerman

Become a big Twitter fish.

In this day and age, cultivating a large set of Twitter followers isn't just a vanity project; it's an asset. Followers can be mobilized for important causes, retweeting your message and amplifying it across the Twittersphere.

Jenny Soep

Vote, vote, vote.

"BE THE CHANGE
THAT YOU WISH
TO SEE IN THE
WORLD"
M. GANDHI

JENNY SOEP

If everybody who could vote did vote, it would change the world. In the United States, around 40 percent or more of eligible voters don't vote in presidential elections. In the United Kingdom, around 33 percent typically don't vote in general elections, while approximately 28 percent didn't take part in the 2016 European Union referendum, or Brexit.

If it's difficult for you to get to the polling station, that's all the more reason to try harder: Politicians don't make laws to please the populations they know won't be voting for them. This leads to poor representation for, say, disabled people or those in rural areas. So, if you only commit to one political action in any given year, make it to vote, vote, vote.

Adrien Lee

Pop your bubble.

Social media platforms like Twitter and Facebook foster "echo chambers" where everyone in the same network shares broadly similar views. This insularity is one reason for the increasingly divided nature of society and politics today. When we only talk and listen to people who agree with us, it can be hard to understand or feel connected to those who have different perspectives. Avoid this by popping your social media bubble. This is easy—just seek out communities, Twitter feeds, subreddits, and Facebook groups that reflect communities other than your own.

Face your nemesis.

If you really want to challenge your own viewpoint, seek out someone who holds the opposite view and invite them for a respectful discussion. The purpose isn't to spark a fight or to prove that you're right, but to see if, by talking and listening to the "other side," you might better understand their point of view and find common ground. This is a way to test your own blindspots and biases and to try to discover new perspectives. Even if this only confirms your beliefs, that can lend further courage to your convictions. And you never know: There's a chance that, by talking to your nemesis, you might both find common ground.

Get off your arse.

Get, get, get get

Get, get, get get

Get, get, get get

Get, get, get get

Get off your arse!

Get off your arse!

Get off your arse!

Get off your arse!

Get off your arse!

Get off your arse and do something good for the world.

Get off your knees and STAND up,
Let's take back the world.

Form a choir, sing this song, make a noise

Get,get,get,get,get,get,get,get   Get,get,get,get,get,get,get,get

1. Get off your arse. Get off your arse. Get off your arse. Get off your arse.

2. Get off your arse. Get off your arse. Get off your arse. Get off your arse.

1 & 2. Get off your arse and do something good for the world.

3 & 4. Get off your arse and do something good for the world.

Words and music by Boff Whalley
for Commoners Choir

Pictures @thingsbyuna

Everybody, sing along! "Get, get, get, get. Get, get, get, get. . . ." Campaign, march, demonstrate, vote, petition, fundraise, support, volunteer, and take direct action. Identify one thing you'd like to change. One problem that needs to be solved. One person who needs help. One community that lacks a voice. Then form a choir, sing this song, and make a noise.

Richy K. Chandler

Do your research.

When trying to help others, always ask what people need and want first. After all, they'll know best! Many well-intentioned folk make assumptions about what other people need—or how to solve a problem—and it turns out they are mistaken. People might not want the particular type of help being offered, or it might not in fact be useful. Trying to help in the wrong way can sometimes even make things worse.

Hannah McCann

Know your representatives.

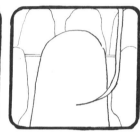

KNOW YOUR REPRESENTATIVES

IF YOU HAVE ACCESS TO THE INTERNET, YOU CAN FIND OUT WHO REPRESENTS YOU IN NATIONAL GOVERNMENT. YOU CAN ALSO ASSESS HOW WELL THEY ARE DOING THEIR JOB.

OH, IT'S YOU

SOME OF THE TRANSCRIPTS CAN BE LONG, BORING, AND DIFFICULT TO FOLLOW. BUT FROM THEM WE CAN GET A BETTER PICTURE OF THEIR IDEALS AND THEIR ABILITY TO STAND UP FOR THEM.

COFFEE

THINGS TO LOOK AT:

WHAT THEY VOTED ON, AND HOW THEY VOTED.

WHAT THEY CLAIM AS EXPENSES.

£ £ £ HMM...

WHAT EXACTLY THEY SAY.

GOOD LUCK!

Get to know the people who have been elected to represent you. Knowledge is power. Learn the names of your representatives in local, state, and national government, visit their websites, sign up for their newsletters, and track their votes. This will help you decide if you want them reelected, and if you write to them, you can speak knowledgeably about what they've done (and not done).

Henri Tervapuro

Meme it up.

If you want to get people's attention about something politically outrageous, world-changing, or important, ain't nothing like a meme to get it out there. Visit a meme generating website, stick it on Twitter or Facebook, and see what happens.

Pete Renshaw

Put your money where your mouth is.

Ever heard the old adage "Be the change you want to see in the world"? Or "Walk the walk, don't just talk the talk"? The point is, if you believe good causes need support, then do your part to support good causes. Take some of your own income—or if you own a business, take some of its profits—and donate them. It doesn't really matter how much you give, just give something.

Lily-Rose Beardshaw

Organize a charity event.

If you want to raise funds for a good cause, organize a charity event to generate donations from the community. Any kind of event can work: Create an old-fashioned bake sale, get your artist friends to donate a piece of work for an auction, or arrange a performance night. Not only will you collect much-needed cash, you'll raise awareness for a cause that needs it.

Paul Shinn

Donate your castoffs.

Don't want it and don't need it? Don't trash it! Many services exist that take used or broken goods and clothes, clean and refurbish them, and donate them (or the proceeds from sales) to charity. People without any phone might welcome last year's model, and even if your car is only good for scrap, that scrap has value. Finding new homes for unwanted castoffs is part of the "reduce, reuse, recycle" ethic.

Jenny Drew

Create community.

It's easy to feel isolated and alone, especially when circumstances are difficult. To avoid that, look for ways to create community within the context of your life. Have you picked up some practical knowledge along the way? Consider multiplying its effect by sharing with your community. Some people will appreciate picking up tips about gardening, cooking, bike repair, yoga, or whatever.

Try organizing a rotating potluck dinner or creating a neighborhood gardening club. Then, if you like, this same community can be galvanized to enact social and political change in your wider community.

Victor Szepessy

Watch your words.

Be aware of the words you, and others, use to describe people of different ethnicities, cultures, races, abilities, genders, and so on. Ideally, use the terms and language that they use to talk about themselves. If you don't know, ask or find out. And when you notice biased language in the media, speak out against it.

Latina journalist Daisy Hernández, author of the memoir *A Cup of Water Under My Bed*, says, "What are you noticing about headlines when the police kill another Black teenager? Is the teen described as a kid on his way to college or as a 'Black male'? I try to raise awareness that we're trafficking in racial ideology 24/7 online—and that we can change the direction of these conversations every time we hit comment."

Support a food drive.

Fighting hunger within your community might be one of the simplest ways to combine compassion and politics since it directly improves lives and fights poverty. The best place to start is by contacting your local or regional food bank: They can provide running lists of the kinds of food they need, and they are equipped to distribute it.

All you need to do is collect and deliver the food. Ask your neighbors to help, or convince local schools, kids' sports teams, and businesses to sponsor a drive. If you turn it into a contest, seeing which team can come up with the most goods, you'll tap into the competitive instinct and really maximize the benefits!

Sally Kindberg

Expand your kids' world.

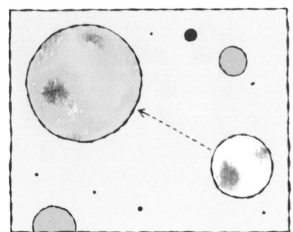

© Sally Kindberg

Make sure your children are reading books and watching movies that present a diverse range of characters and expose them to worlds outside their own. Choose entertainment that helps them grow up to be world citizens.

David Baillie

Be a witness.

Being a witness is one of the most powerful ways to bring light to a problem: It just means sharing what you observe about a situation, conflict, or confrontation. This has never been easier or more important than today, when smartphones and social media allow anyone to take photos, record videos, and post observations of events in real time. This visual evidence can right wrongs and bring justice. Examples are everywhere, but consider the importance of bystander recordings of the murder by police of George Floyd in 2020 and the storming of the US Capitol in January 2021. Be a witness, and share what you see.

Abigail Lingford

Plant a tree.

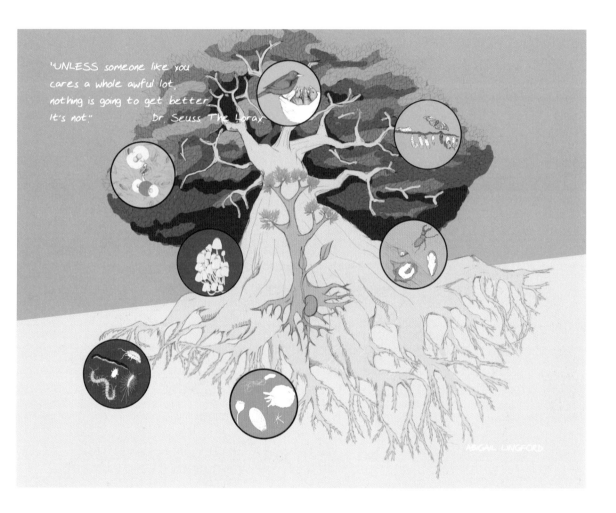

"UNLESS someone like you cares a whole awful lot, nothing is going to get better. It's not." — Dr. Seuss The Lorax

It's a simple equation: Adding trees benefits the world and subtracting trees does not. So plant a tree—or better yet, a forest. You can take this literally, by bringing a shovel and a sapling to your own backyard, or by donating money to organizations that plant where needed.

Trees provide food and shelter for wildlife, and they can improve soils, fight erosion, mitigate flooding, and absorb carbon dioxide to help curb climate change. Most of all? Trees feel good! Being in green spaces improves our mood and well-being. For help planting trees—either where you live or around the world—contact the Nature Conservancy or the UK Woodland Trust.

Amplify your voice.

Despite progress, women and minorities still face discrimination and inequality in the workplace. One strategy for combating this and making sure everyone is being heard is called "amplification."

This was a deliberate, regular practice by female White House staffers during Barack Obama's first term as US president. In meetings, when one woman made a key point or suggestion, other women repeated it and credited its originator. Over time, this forced male staff to recognize the contributions of women and listen to them more often. In a predominately white, male-dominated culture or workplace, one that muffles other opinions and issues, practice amplification and be heard.

Beth Zyglowicz

Find your comfort zone.

Any organization or political action requires a range of different skills. To be effective, it doesn't make sense for everyone to do the same thing, and besides, not everyone is good at everything. So find your comfort zone and help in the ways that fit you best. Some people are made for the frontlines; they love to lead the charge. Others prefer to stay in the background and provide support—cooking food, making signs, and cheering others. Everyone is essential, so help in the ways you can.

Myfanwy Tristram

Travel more slowly.

Of course, everyone today is in a hurry—everyone wants to move fast—but traveling more slowly can help save the planet. Rather than drive or fly to your destination—two modes of transportation that create the most pollution—take some extra time and go by train, boat, bus, or bicycle instead. Taking fewer flights can be a reward in itself, since it turns the journey into its own memorable adventure.

Guin Thompson

Invest in your community.

credit unions help your community blossom

Corporate banks, like any private business, seek to make profits. They use your money to make money by investing deposits in other enterprises. Do you know what your bank invests in? Find out, and if they fund things you don't like—say, fossil fuels, extraction industries, arms manufacturing, and so on—find a new bank. And tell your old bank, "It's not me, it's you."

One banking alternative is a credit union. These are nonprofit cooperatives run by and for their members. Their goal is solely to benefit members with lower fees and affordable loans, and members themselves vote on how to invest, typically choosing projects in the local community. In other words, credit unions help sow green with your green.

Miia Vistilä

Listen with an open mind.

Finding the best way to help and support others can be difficult in any situation. Yet it can be especially hard when we don't personally have direct experience of whatever issue someone is dealing with. When you're uncertain of what to do or say, the best approach is often to let the other person be your guide. Ask them if they want to talk, and if so, listen with an open mind and seek to understand their experience. If they don't want to talk, respect that choice while extending your offer to help if they want it.

Graeme McGregor

Reread history.

They say history is written by the victors, so a great way to understand the roots of injustice is to read accounts written by or about everyday people—the disenfranchised, the powerless, the losers, the enslaved and oppressed. Try historian Henry Reynolds's *The Other Side of the Frontier*, about indigenous peoples in Australia, or Howard Zinn's *A People's History of the United States*. Memoirs and biographies are also excellent windows into overlooked experiences: Maybe begin with *I Know Why the Caged Bird Sings* by Maya Angelou, *Black Elk Speaks* by John Neihardt, *The Autobiography of Malcolm X*, and any others that tell stories that might not have been part of your school curriculum.

Eat less meat.

SAVES FORESTS

FORESTS ARE DESTROYED TO MAKE ROOM FOR LIVESTOCK.

REDUCES POLLUTION

LIVESTOCK PRODUCES 14.5% OF THE WORLDS GREENHOUSE GASES.

USES LESS WATER

IT TAKES A LOT LESS WATER TO GROW GRAINS, BEANS LEGUMES AND VEG.

SARAH LIPPETT

Raising livestock for meat, especially cattle, is taking a serious toll on our planet. Producers destroy forests to create more grazing land. They use up sometimes scarce water resources, much more than are needed to grow vegetables and grains, which would feed more people.

Livestock also produce tons of waste that can cause all sorts of environmental damage; cow burps release massive amounts of methane, one of the most harmful greenhouse gases. Eating less meat, or going vegetarian, is good for the planet, and it's healthier, too.

Create a barter economy.

Save some money and make new friends by bartering your skills and services. Trade someone's babysitting help for your carpentry skills, or organize the neighbors to help with big projects, like an old-fashioned "barn raising." Friendly bartering helps build friendly communities.

Switch to green.

Aki Alaraatikka

Replacing fossil fuels with renewable energy sources is an essential step in humanity's push to mitigate climate change. We can each do our part by switching to a green energy provider for our homes. This ensures that the electricity that charges our phones and provides heat and light is produced by wind, sun, and sea. Swapping providers is really easy these days, and you'll feel better and make a proper difference every time you boil the kettle—but do your homework and make sure you pick a company that isn't just "greenwashing," or using eco buzzwords to make them sound cleaner than they really are.

Beata Sosnowska

Help out refugees.

BEATA SOSNOWSKA

When we think of volunteering, we usually think of ways to help people who already live in our own communities. But also consider helping immigrants who are seeking new places to live, particularly refugees fleeing persecution, who often need the most help. Check the websites of refugee-focused organizations to see what these groups need, but they often can use help sorting donations and packing aid. For those who can travel, there are usually openings to help distribute goods to other places or in other countries.

Jacqueline Nicholls

Crank up the Singer.

If you aren't already handy with a sewing machine, it's never too late to learn. Making your own clothes and having the skills to repair used clothing are good ways to save money, minimize the impact of consumerism, and look good while doing it. It's self-expression that makes a statement. After all, why always buy new clothes? That only supports the international fashion industry—which often exploits workers, ships garments halfway around the world, and dictates styles and trends. Start your own fashion industry of one.

Question the new norms.

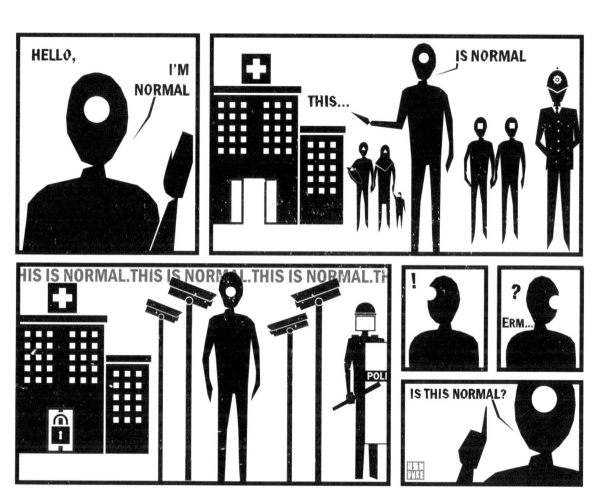

One role of government is to provide vital public services that support all of society. While every country defines this differently, it typically includes hospitals and health care; libraries, schools, and education; infrastructure; public safety; child care and family support; programs to help the poor; and much more.

When government cuts these programs or slashes support, this risks creating a "new normal" in which people accept living with less or even living without. Don't let that happen. Put pressure on government to restore or continue the essential social programs upon which society depends.

Buy clothes that last.

THE ACTIVIST GUIDE TO A LONG, FABULOUS LIFE for your clothes

BUY SMART · ETHICAL · VERSATILE · VINTAGE · QUALITY ·

refashion & restyle

REPAIR

RECYCLE · SELL · CHARITY · SWAP · GIFT · REPURPOSE ·

RICA MARCH · 2017

"Fast fashion" is the phenomenon of cheap trendy shops churning out designer-style clothes that are only made to last a season, cost almost nothing, and then end up in a landfill. This practice is bad for the environment and bad for workers, since it encourages sweatshops. Only by using cheap labor and cheap materials can retailers afford to sell cheap clothes.

Resist the lure of fast fashion. Research ethical companies and take your business there, and then take care of your clothes so they last longer. Even if you buy fewer items, they will be of higher quality, and you'll feel better in them.

Send a letter of comfort.

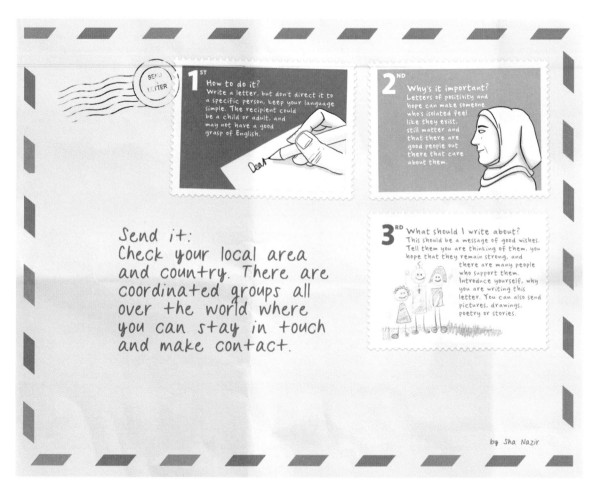

1ST How to do it?
Write a letter, but don't direct it to a specific person, keep your language simple. The recipient could be a child or adult, and may not have a good grasp of English.

2ND Why's it important?
Letters of positivity and hope can make someone who's isolated feel like they exist, still matter and that there are good people out there that care about them.

Send it:
Check your local area and country. There are coordinated groups all over the world where you can stay in touch and make contact.

3RD What should I write about?
This should be a message of good wishes. Tell them you are thinking of them, you hope that they remain strong, and there are many people who support them. Introduce yourself, why you are writing this letter. You can also send pictures, drawings, poetry or stories.

by Sha Nazir

Refugees fleeing danger in their home country and seeking a new place to live become known as asylum seekers when they arrive in a new land. They are typically held in detention centers as they wait for their asylum petitions to be reviewed and then approved or not—sometimes for months or even years. Annually around the world, about a million people seek asylum.

What can you do? Write a letter to someone being held in detention, so they feel less isolated and alone. Contact a refugee agency for help with what to write and how to coordinate delivery of a message of hope, comfort, and kindness.

Hannah Berry

Interpret a new life.

If you're bilingual, your language skills could be of great help to immigrants who are settling in your country. Contact an immigrant charity to volunteer your interpreter skills or to translate the printed materials that help service users understand the new culture they're now part of, what services are available, and how to apply for them.

Donate skills.

Dave Windett (Text by John Gatehouse)

When it comes to volunteering, get creative! Donations can include much more than money. Consider all the practical ways you can help charities, especially if you have specific skills like bookkeeping, carpentry, plumbing, computer coding, art design, writing, managing social media, and so on. If you're a lawyer, offer pro bono legal help. Whatever you're good at, there's an organization that will be glad of it.

Mirka Oinonen

Smile, don't stare.

It's common courtesy, something your parents always told you: It's not polite to stare. That doesn't change just because someone looks different—they're still a human being with feelings. Imagine the situation reversed. How would you feel? So smile, don't stare, and see the person, not the difference.

One of our artists says, "I'm a wheelchair user and get stared at a lot, but those who just nod, smile, and acknowledge me make my day."

Beth Dawson

Promote a living wage.

" For many, rather than being the lowest rung on the ladder, low pay is a life-long existence that passes from generation to generation. "

THE LIVING WAGE COMMISSION

In many countries, the legally required "minimum wage" is not enough to live on, and people in low-wage jobs are often unable to meet their own or their family's basic needs. Instead, the minimum wage needs to be increased so that it becomes a "living wage," which is whatever provides enough income to afford a basic standard of living.

So support efforts to raise the minimum wage— to fight poverty and income inequality—and if you run a business, make an effort to pay employees a living wage. (This rate varies of course depending on location.) You'll nurture happier, more engaged workers who are more likely to stick around, which saves recruitment and onboarding costs in the long term, and creates a more positive workplace.

Maël Estevez

Write (and share) music.

If music is your superpower, use it. Write songs that capture your political message. Remember: The catchier the tune, the more likely it is to spread. Not a musician? Promote and recommend those artists who sing about what you think people need to hear.

Take a cue from the Argentine fact-checking service Chequeado. They created a hummable, Spanish-language tune called "Paren el Guitarreo"—which roughly translates as "stop the lies"—and fashioned a humorous viral video mocking the country's dishonest politicians.

Tell stories.

Personal stories show the human side of big issues and illustrate why politics and social justice matter. They go straight to the heart. If you're a natural yarn spinner, use your storytelling skills to share the experiences of those who are affected by political decisions or natural disasters, and help them get their insights into the public eye.

If you've got skills in writing, video, or recording, so much the better. And if you haven't, what better time to learn? These days, there are so many opportunities to share stories—on YouTube, blogs, podcasts, or even good old-fashioned print media—and there's always room for some new voices explaining experiences that might not be known or fully understood by the population at large.

Broadcast your message.

Radio and podcasts are a great way to tell stories and get your message across—right into people's ears! Sound is one of the most direct and intimate forms of media.

Is there a community radio station near you, and would they accept, for example, a program full of refugee voices, or political debates featuring those most affected by the latest changes to the law? You'll find hosting a show is much less intimidating than you might think, once you get started: Interviewing people is nothing more than having an interesting conversation about an important topic.

If you can't find a radio station, how about doing it yourself and putting out a podcast? Starting up requires a small amount of research, know-how, and time, but you don't need sophisticated, expensive equipment—you can speak to the world right from your own garage or closet.

Call it out.

The internet and social media mean never having to suffer in silence. If you experience bias, hate, abuse, or disrespect—whether online or off—there's the option to call it out in public. A number of Twitter and Instagram accounts and some websites already encourage this. The Everyday Sexism project's website and the Bye Felipe Instagram account allow women to share experiences of sexism and misogyny, and the For Exposure Twitter account exposes requests that artists work for free.

This simple, effective strategy calls attention to bad behavior that society often ignores. Can't find a social media account that tackles a particular injustice? Copy this model and set up your own.

Forage for dinner.

Even in the city, foraging is a way to find great food. It's the ultimate approach for reducing your food-related carbon footprint—plus you save money, get exercise, and reconnect with the natural world. In Europe, people still sometimes use truffle pigs to sniff out wild truffles, but if you don't have a pet pig at hand, you might need more help to forage safely. Take a course to make sure you're picking the right plants—and avoiding poisonous toadstools.

Jaime Huxtable

Build a wall of kindness.

In the winter of 2015, an anonymous person built a "wall of kindness" in Mashhad, Iran. Along a stretch of repainted wall furnished with pegs, people were encouraged to hang clothes, food, and goods for the homeless or poor to take. Written on the wall was the motto "Leave what you don't need. Take what you do."

The concept quickly spread throughout Iran and to Pakistan, India, Jordan, China, Italy, Britain, and more. Consider starting a wall of kindness where you live to encourage the community to help those most in need.

Riyadh Rateme

Don't waste food.

Food waste is a serious global problem, one that goes beyond cleaning your plate. Every year in America, nearly 40 percent of food is thrown away, creating billions of pounds in waste that impacts the environment. Meanwhile, people without enough food to begin with are going hungry. The trick is getting all that still-good-but-unwanted food to them.

That's where charities like Feeding America, Love Food Hate Waste, and the Real Junk Food Project come in. They coordinate with local restaurants and stores to donate their surplus or leftover food to the homeless. Contact these groups to help rescue and distribute food or to set up local programs. Then promote international Stop Food Waste Day, every April 28!

Beata Sosnowska

Take back the night.

Everyone should feel free to walk where they want, when they want; however, as many women will tell you, they don't, particularly walking alone at night.

Take Back the Night marches—also called Reclaim the Night in England, Australia, and some other countries—are organized to raise awareness about and fight to end sexual assault and violence against women. Send a message of support loud and clear by joining one of these marches where you live, which sometimes take over the same streets and parks where women have experienced violence and feel unsafe. Men are often welcome, but some marches only invite women.

89

Sharon Lee De La Cruz

Don't take it on.

Trying to do our part to improve the world can feel overwhelming at times. We can become discouraged, anxious, or depressed, especially when change is slow or seemingly nonexistent.

Recognize these feelings when they occur. They're part of the wardrobe of being human. Just remember, you can choose what to wear.

Bishakh Som

Put your phone down.

Communications technology is a very powerful tool for fostering connection. In fact, only one thing is more powerful: real life. Being in the world, talking in person, sharing an embrace, plugging into nature and not a device. When you really want to connect, whether inside yourself or with others, put the phone down and meet IRL.

Jim Terry

Remember the past.

As the old saying goes, those who don't learn from history are destined to repeat it. Think the wars, greed, and prejudices of today are brand-new? Study the past in order to see connections with the present, which can help us understand and stop devastating cycles of conflict and oppression.

Tracy White

Listen to refugees.

"TWO OF OUR KIDS WERE KIDNAPPED BY A CARTEL. THEY CALLED DEMANDING RANSOM".

HE WAS A FISHERMAN.

"I COULD HEAR OUR DAUGHTERS IN THE BACKGROUND. [THE GUY] SAID, WHOSE FINGERS SHOULD WE CHOP OFF FIRST SO YOU BELIEVE WE'RE SERIOUS?"

HIS WIFE OWNED A STORE.

"THEY GOT REALLY ANGRY BECAUSE OUR KIDS ESCAPED SO THEY DIDN'T HAVE THE MONEY. THEY SAID THEY'D KILL MY WIFE AND HER SISTER".

HE HID WITH HIS FAMILY.

"I WENT TO THE POLICE. THE POLICE SAID YOU'RE LUCKY, YOUR KIDS ARE ALIVE. IF THEY CALL US WE WILL DETAIN YOU AND BRING YOU WHEREVER THEY SAY.

SO LEAVE NOW".

HE GAVE AN INTERVIEW. MEXICO, 2019.

News about immigration and refugees can seem dry and abstract. It often focuses on numbers and statistics and on the costs for the receiving country. Balance this by learning about the refugees themselves. Seek out and share news and documentaries that tell real stories. Knowing who people are and why they risk their lives to flee terrible circumstances can make it easier to feel compassion and respond with generosity.

Amy Lam

Meet the neighbors.

AMY LAM | MOBILEREPUBLIC.TUMBLR

To connect with your neighborhood, and to help build a sense of community, organize a street party, and meet the folk who live nearby. Encourage your neighbors to get to know one another. Share food, play games, and have fun, and as you do, find opportunities to ask if anyone has concerns that the community could help with. If this becomes a regular thing, you'll find it will make your neighborhood a friendlier, better place to live.

Start a casserole club.

The Casserole Club is an Australian charity that organizes volunteers who, as they say, "share extra portions of home-cooked food with people in their area who aren't always able to cook for themselves." If you're cooking a meal anyway, why not stretch it to one more diner?

Like the more formal Meals on Wheels food-delivery program in America, this primarily helps the elderly, the disabled, and anyone who has trouble leaving the house. It's not only about feeding people; it spreads cheer and combats loneliness, too. Organize your own informal casserole club to help someone you know, or volunteer with a local group to make or deliver food.

Volunteer!

Have you ever considered volunteer work? It's a great way to engage in your community and build your skill set.

Find something you're passionate about. Some common volunteering choices are helping at a food pantry, tutoring and working with the homeless.

If you know of an organization in your area that you'd like to help out at, great! Most can be reached online. If you're unsure where to volunteer, sites like volunteermatch.org can be helpful.

VolunteerMatch.org

It's important to think about how much time you're able to give. It's okay to start small! one or two hours a week is fine, as is one day a month.

Be sure to let the organization that you choose know about any skills you might have. They can give you tasks more suited to you that way.

Be sure to have fun with it! Once you're in the swing of it, you'll love it.

If this book has one key takeaway, it's this: To solve the world's many problems, big and small, everyone needs to get involved. What's the easiest way? Volunteer!

At its simplest, volunteering means dedicating some of your time to help another person in need. For many charities and organizations, time is as precious as money, since everyone's time is limited. If you need help finding the right situation—to make the most of your volunteering time—contact a volunteer match organization, like VolunteerMatch.org or Idealist.org. Their whole purpose is to ensure volunteering is as effective and satisfying as possible.

Go large.

Billboards aren't just for advertisements, and any wall, sidewalk, or street can hold a mural. It might take cash or city planning, but you can splash your message in places and at a size that everyone can see. The 2017 movie *Three Billboards Outside Ebbing, Missouri*—based on a real incident in which someone posted three billboards protesting an unsolved murder—inspired others to create their own protest billboards. In 2020, to accompany protests, muralists painted the phrase "Black Lives Matter" along a Washington, DC, street—in writing so large it can be seen from space. Since then, other cities around the world have copied this.

In the UK, the anti-Brexit group Led by Donkeys rented billboards in towns across the country and used these prominently positioned posters to publicize politicians' hypocrisies. What might you do?

Have your day in court.

Democratic, elected governments are created to serve citizens. When governments don't, or when officials cause harm and break the law, they can be held accountable: You can take them to court. Suing for your rights, and for the rights of all people, takes guts, money, and perseverance, but it can be done.

One recent example is the youth-led climate lawsuit *Juliana v. United States*. Filed in 2015 by Our Children's Trust, a nonprofit law firm, it argues that the US government has "violated the youngest generation's constitutional right" to a healthy environment. Similar climate lawsuits have been filed in every US state and in many other countries. As it turns out, you *can* fight city hall.

Rachael Ball

Be a Raging Granny.

Becoming a grandparent doesn't mean your protesting days are over. On the contrary, much like youths, elders have the time to fight for justice, plus wisdom and humor borne from experience. One example? The Raging Grannies, who formed in Canada in the 1980s and today sponsor "gaggles" across the United States, the United Kingdom, and more.

According to their website, "The delights of grannying include: dressing like innocent little old ladies so we can get close to our 'target,' writing songs from old favorites that skewer modern wrongs, satirizing evil-doing in public and getting everyone singing about it. . . . Grannying is the least understood yet most powerful weapon we have."

Run for office.

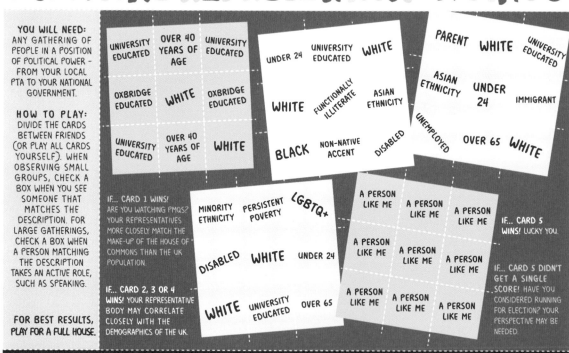

POLITICAL REPRESENTATION BINGO

YOU WILL NEED:
ANY GATHERING OF PEOPLE IN A POSITION OF POLITICAL POWER – FROM YOUR LOCAL PTA TO YOUR NATIONAL GOVERNMENT.

HOW TO PLAY:
DIVIDE THE CARDS BETWEEN FRIENDS (OR PLAY ALL CARDS YOURSELF). WHEN OBSERVING SMALL GROUPS, CHECK A BOX WHEN YOU SEE SOMEONE THAT MATCHES THE DESCRIPTION. FOR LARGE GATHERINGS, CHECK A BOX WHEN A PERSON MATCHING THE DESCRIPTION TAKES AN ACTIVE ROLE, SUCH AS SPEAKING.

FOR BEST RESULTS, PLAY FOR A FULL HOUSE.

IF... CARD 1 WINS!
ARE YOU WATCHING PMQS? YOUR REPRESENTATIVES MORE CLOSELY MATCH THE MAKE-UP OF THE HOUSE OF COMMONS THAN THE UK POPULATION.

IF... CARD 2, 3 OR 4 WINS! YOUR REPRESENTATIVE BODY MAY CORRELATE CLOSELY WITH THE DEMOGRAPHICS OF THE UK.

IF... CARD 5 WINS! LUCKY YOU.

IF... CARD 5 DIDN'T GET A SINGLE SCORE! HAVE YOU CONSIDERED RUNNING FOR ELECTION? YOUR PERSPECTIVE MAY BE NEEDED.

Card 1:
UNIVERSITY EDUCATED	OVER 40 YEARS OF AGE	UNIVERSITY EDUCATED
OXBRIDGE EDUCATED	WHITE	OXBRIDGE EDUCATED
UNIVERSITY EDUCATED	OVER 40 YEARS OF AGE	WHITE

Card 2:
UNDER 24	UNIVERSITY EDUCATED	WHITE
WHITE	FUNCTIONALLY ILLITERATE	ASIAN ETHNICITY
BLACK	NON-NATIVE ACCENT	DISABLED

Card 3:
PARENT	WHITE	UNIVERSITY EDUCATED
ASIAN ETHNICITY	UNDER 24	IMMIGRANT
UNEMPLOYED	OVER 65	WHITE

Card 4:
MINORITY ETHNICITY	PERSISTENT POVERTY	LGBTQ+
DISABLED	WHITE	UNDER 24
WHITE	UNIVERSITY EDUCATED	OVER 65

Card 5:
A PERSON LIKE ME	A PERSON LIKE ME	A PERSON LIKE ME
A PERSON LIKE ME	A PERSON LIKE ME	A PERSON LIKE ME
A PERSON LIKE ME	A PERSON LIKE ME	A PERSON LIKE ME

THESE BINGO CARDS WERE POPULATED THOUGHTFULLY USING BACK-ON-NAPKIN MATHEMATICS. THE GOOD REPUTATION OF SOURCES SUCH AS PARLIAMENT. CO.UK AND THE ONS HAVE BEEN UNFAIRLY BESMIRCHED IN THE PROCESS. CARDS 2, 3 AND 4 WERE POPULATED TOGETHER AS ONE 'WHOLE'; EACH REPRESENTS ONLY A FLAVOUR OF THE UK POPULATION ALONE. I DID NOT AIM FOR PROPORTIONAL RELATIONSHIPS BETWEEN THE SIZES OF GROUPS. I STRONGLY ENCOURAGE YOU TO ADAPT THESE CARDS TO YOUR LOCAL POPULATION. – R. DEVINE

Don't just protest the government from the outside, become part of it and effect change from within. By running for office, you can raise awareness about important issues, and if you win a seat, you can directly ensure that all people and communities are represented and served. When government is dominated by rich white men—or any privileged group—it's no surprise that legislation so often favors them. Represent yourself and your community and run for local, state, or even national office.

Jan Wheatley

Don't join the circus.

The world is full of distractions and reasons not to take action, and the powers that be like it that way. It suits corporations when the marketplace and the media become a circus sideshow of entertainments, dire warnings, despair, and confusion. This leads people to think that trying to change things for the better is a waste of time.

Don't join that circus. Gather together—online or in your living room—and make a plan for what you want to achieve. Becoming united with others in a common cause is the best way to stay motivated and productive.

Kate Moon

Encourage someone's voice.

Some people have a hard time being heard. They live quietly and their voices are easily drowned out, such as those with learning difficulties, the frail, the elderly, and so on. If you know or meet someone like this, reach out, ask how they are doing, and see if they need help.

Everyone appreciates having someone who listens and takes an interest, but people might also need an advocate to help them deal with landlords, banks, utilities, and other institutions that won't listen. Encourage or be someone's voice.

Teach a language.

You don't have to speak another language to help people who are learning to speak yours. If you know someone who is new to your native language, take the time to help them learn—and you can pick up some of that person's language in the bargain! Helping teach newly arrived immigrants or refugees how to get to grips with their new language is also an excellent volunteer opportunity.

Be a mentor.

Be a mentor to a young person in need of guidance, companionship, or help navigating a difficult stage of life. You can volunteer through an organization like Big Brothers Big Sisters, which matches you with a disadvantaged youth so you can help them realize their potential. Big Brothers has chapters in many countries, and local charities may also sponsor mentoring programs in your region.

Zara Slattery

Plant radical roots.

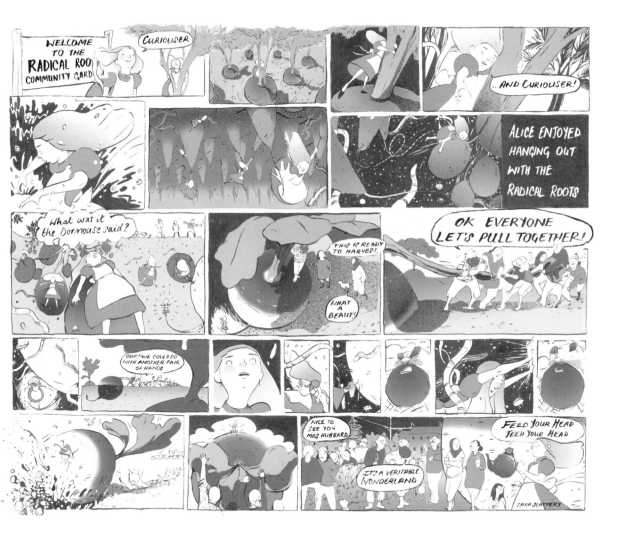

Start a community gardening project where everyone reaps what you sow together. As you grow cheap, healthy food, you also create friendships, get fresh air and exercise, improve your mental health, boost the local ecosystem, and reduce your carbon footprint since the fruit and vegetables you harvest don't need to travel halfway around the world to reach your table. Plus, wouldn't we all benefit from a new green area in the neighborhood?

Nic Vas

Stand up for immigrants.

Stand up for the rights of immigrants to be treated humanely. This starts by avoiding the disparaging, dehumanizing label "illegal immigrant." Immigrants might be "undocumented" or "unauthorized to be in a country," but they remain human beings deserving of dignity and respect. For many, their only desire is to live safely and become fellow citizens.

Speak out against anti-immigrant government policies and harmful treatment. Protest detention centers that crowd people in unsafe, unsanitary conditions, and take action when agencies threaten to make widespread arrests through immigration raids. Some groups don't just voice solidarity: They link arms to block federal agents. That sort of direct confrontation isn't for everyone, but it's not the only way to stand up for immigrants.

Kirsty Hunter

Rewire the grid.

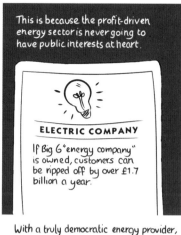

: KIRSTY HUNTER :

To shrink their carbon footprint, some people go "off the grid" by generating their own power. A more transformative approach might be remaking the grid itself as a member-owned community cooperative.

One example is People's Energy in Scotland. This nonprofit electricity provider is devoted to both renewable energy and social justice. They pledge to give 75 percent of their profits back to customers to provide "electricity that's clean as well as kind."

What if every electric company made that pledge? What if every bank, public transportation, and mobile phone company was owned by the people it served, making decisions based on their needs rather than the need for profit? Now that would make those monthly utility bills a little more welcome.

Karen Rubins

Become a community sponsor.

When refugees flee to a new country, they need all the help they can get. While national governments run refugee resettlement programs, one of the most effective ways to integrate refugees into new lives is through "community sponsorship." This is when individuals or groups volunteer to support refugee families in their own communities.

In Britain, the national government runs a "Community Sponsors" program, and in the United States, the Refugee Council USA provides this assistance. In many ways, this is a life-saving service, so consider providing this welcome for people seeking happier, safer, more successful lives.

Joan Reilly

Embrace craftivism.

Craft is a tangible means of communication,

EYE-CATCHING, HANDMADE VISUAL DISPLAYS HELPED THE WOMEN'S SUFFRAGE MOVEMENT TO SWAY PUBLIC OPINION TOWARD GRANTING WOMEN THE RIGHT TO VOTE.

THE PORTABLE SPINNING WHEEL INVENTED BY MOHANDAS GANDHI HELPED TO INSPIRE CITIZENS OF INDIA TO BECOME ECONOMICALLY INDEPENDENT FROM THE BRITISH GOVERNMENT.

THE AIDS MEMORIAL QUILT BY THE NAMES PROJECT CONFRONTED THE WORLD WITH THE ENORMITY OF LOSS BEING CAUSED BY THE DISEASE, AND HELPED TO BRING IT THE ATTENTION IT DESERVED.

THE HANDKERCHIEF CAMPAIGN BY SARAH CORBETT'S CRAFTIVIST COLLECTIVE SPOKE TO M&S EXECUTIVES ON A PERSONAL LEVEL AND MOVED THEM TO PAY THEIR EMPLOYEES A HIGHER WAGE.

and thus a powerful tool for creating political change.

What do you get when you combine needlepoint with activism? Craftivism, of course! People have been stitching their protests for centuries, from suffragettes' slogans to the community-stitched AIDS quilt and trade unions' intricately embroidered banners. You, too, can use handicrafts to change our world.

Sarah Corbett, founder of the UK-based Craftivist Collective, understands that quiet, nonconfrontational defiance can be as effective as loud marches in the street. She led the 2015 project to give embroidered handkerchiefs to the board of the Marks & Spencer department store chain to convince them to pay their 50,000 employees a living wage, and it worked. As the Craftivist Collective manifesto states, "If we want our world to be more beautiful, kind, and just, then let's make our activism beautiful, kind, and just."

109

Steve Reynolds

Hack your streets.

When cutbacks to local services mean that basic street maintenance and neighborhood repairs are being neglected, what can you do? Here's a radical idea—fix it yourself! Naturally, hacking your streets isn't always strictly legal, so know your local laws and whether your neighborhood beautification efforts might run afoul of city ordinances. Maybe citizens are allowed to fill minor potholes in your area, and maybe not. But if planting flowers, fixing signs, mowing medians, and removing trash is wrong, do you wanna be right?

Practice shop dropping.

Shop dropping is the opposite of shoplifting, and it's a far more satisfying option for activists. Instead of taking from a store, you leave a little something as a political message for future shoppers to find. Perhaps slip a note into a jacket pocket about the manufacturer's use of sweatshops, or leave a drawing between the pages of a book. Place a Post-it over a price tag, explaining the real costs of the item (in terms of carbon emissions, sweatshop labor, or social inequality). Spread messages that need to be seen, leaving them in places where people least expect them . . . but maybe don't hit the same store twice.

Wallis Eates

See people's potential.

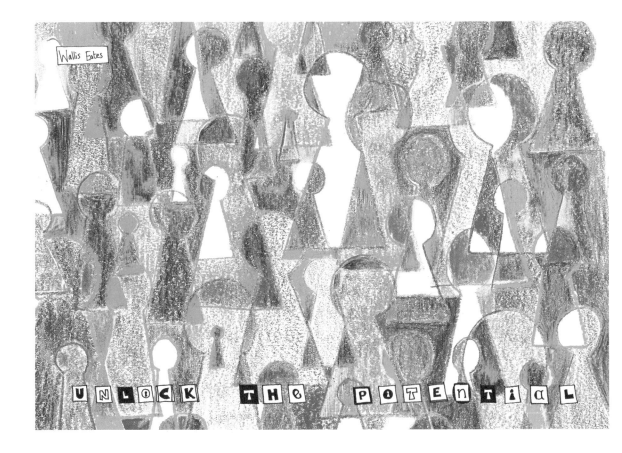

If you run your own business or hire employees, consider hiring those who might find it hard to secure work in traditional jobs or workplaces. This helps people help themselves, providing paid work and opportunities for growth that they might not get otherwise.

For instance, consider recruiting from groups such as ex-convicts, or reaching out to immigrant-advocacy groups or organizations that help the poor find employment. Or create jobs specifically designed for those with autism, learning difficulties, or other disabilities. Who knows how much untapped potential you might unlock?

Katriona Chapman

Leave water.

Illustration: Katriona Chapman

Humanitarian organizations like Border Angels and No More Deaths take direct action to help prevent undocumented immigrants from dying of exposure as they try to cross the US/Mexico border. One approach involves leaving jugs of water, nonperishable food, and other supplies along known migrant paths in the desert.

In the United States, leaving water is legal, though volunteers risk arrest for other reasons, like trespassing on private property. For some, providing humanitarian aid and helping save lives is worth that risk.

James Wilkinson

Donate your art.

If you're a visual artist, let the artists in this book inspire you: Use your medium to convey your message, and donate your skills for charity. Help nonprofit organizations by designing their logos, or create illustrations or comics they can use in their marketing and promotion. Photographers can document volunteers in action, and the good their work does, to inspire others.

Jeroen Janssen

Let enough be enough.

Economic equality, social justice, and environmental sustainability are complex, interwoven issues. This includes both defining what qualifies as "justice" and "sustainable" as well as figuring out how to achieve these things. Yet in everyday life, we can measure our actions by a simple yardstick. If we all took only what we needed, only what was "enough" and no more, then everyone might have enough. Then we might not overconsume and harm the environment. If we practice fairness and balance today, we increase the chances that we'll experience fairness and balance tomorrow.

Break the law.

Civil disobedience takes many forms. It ranges from peaceful, nonviolent protests to direct actions that deliberately harm property or disrupt society in the name of ending injustice, saving lives, or improving society. Historically, when situations have gotten bad enough, people have chosen to block bridges, trespass, stand before tanks, obstruct the police, monkey wrench pipelines, cut fishing nets and fences,

blow the whistle on corruption, and otherwise cause a ruckus in order to create change. Sometimes, these actions have led to arrests, fines, and imprisonment, but these were considered worthwhile risks to help achieve justice and desperately needed progress.

Breaking the law has consequences, but sometimes, so does not breaking it.

It takes a village.

The UK version of *Draw the Line* was coordinated by Myfanwy Tristram with practical and emotional support from Karrie Fransman, Michi Mathias, Graeme McGregor, Zara Slattery, Martin Wright, and the production/design skills of Simon Russell and Woodrow Phoenix. This edition that you are holding in your hands is the result of Myfanwy's collaboration with Liz Frances at Street Noise Books, along with the expert writing and editing skills of Jeff Campbell. And thanks to Susan Neuhaus for managing the design production.

It would not have been possible without the generosity of the 106 artists from 16 countries who rose to the challenge of depicting these positive political actions in comic form, and gave their time and talent for free. *Draw the Line* was conceived at a singular time in world politics, and forged an equally remarkable feeling of purpose and hope, which we hope will continue to live on in the activism it inspires.

Thanks are also due to everyone who helped spread the word about the project. And last but not least, every single person who helped this book come into being. Your support has created this publication, which we hope will spark a wave of activism around the world. It has also allowed us to contribute to the charity Choose Love, which helps refugees and displaced people. This charity was chosen by the artists' consensus and reflects *Draw the Line's* core values of getting up and doing something to change the world.

Choose Love.

The *Draw the Line* artists all have agreed to donate their proceeds from the sale of this book to Choose Love, a nonprofit organization helping refugees and displaced people around the world. Choose Love does whatever it takes to provide refugees and displaced people with everything from lifesaving search-and-rescue boats to food and legal advice. They elevate the voices and visibility of refugees and galvanize public support for agile community organizations providing vital support to refugees along migration routes globally. By buying this book you are contributing directly to people who need help—so you see, you're already taking positive political action!

Who drew the lines?

Abigail Lingford	63
Adrien Lee	49
Aki Alaraatikka	72
Al Davison	9
Amanda Priebe	28
Amber Hsu	98
Amy Lam	94
Aneurin (Nye) Wright	44
Apila Pepita Miettinen	85
Ash Pure	75
Beata Sosnowska	73, 89
Beth Dawson	81
Beth Zyglowicz	65
Birta Thrastardottir	11
Bishakh Som	91
Cesar Lador	13
Christine Wong	22
Daniel Locke	37
Danny Noble	14
Dave McKean	39
Dave Windett	79
David Baillie	62
Deborah Fajerman	47
Edie Owczarek-Palfreyman	71, 86
Emily Haworth-Booth	34
Emmi Bat	46
Freya Harrison	35
Fumio Obata	60
Graeme McGregor	69
Guin Thompson	67
Hannah Berry	78
Hannah McCann	53
Henri Tervapuro	54
H-P Lehkonen	24
Hunt Emerson	97
Jacqueline Nicholls	74

Jaime Huxtable	87
James Wilkinson	114
Jan Wheatley	101
Jenny Drew	58
Jenny Soep	48
Jeroen Janssen	41, 115
Jessica Trevino	83
Jim Medway	12
Jim Terry	92
Jo Harrison	4
Joan Reilly	109
Joanna Neary	16
Joe Decie	29
John Riordan	50
Josie Pearse	23
Kane Lynch	103
Karen Rubins	108
Kate Charlesworth	111
Kate Evans	116
Kate Moon	102
Katriona Chapman	113
Keijo Ahlqvist	40
Kirsty Hunter	107
Kripa Joshi	27
Landis Blair	20
Laura Sorvala	95
Lily-Rose Beardshaw	56
Lucy Knisley	3
Maël Estevez	82
Maria Björklund	32
Michi Mathias	84
Miia Vistilä	68
Mijal Bloch	10
Mirka Oinonen	80
Myfanwy Tristram	19, 66
Nate Macabuag	42

Nic Vas	106
Nicholas Sputnik Miller	1
Paul Shinn	57
Pete Renshaw	55
Rachael Ball	99
Rachael House	6
Rakel Stammer	26
Rica March	76
Richard Tingley	17
Richy K. Chandler	21, 52
Riyadh Rateme	88
Roger Langridge	8
Rosa Devine	25, 100
Sally Kindberg	61
Sally-Anne Hickman	18
Sarah Lippett	70
Sarah Mirk	38
Sean Azzopardi	2
Sha Nazir	77
Sharon Lee De La Cruz	90
Siiri Viljakka	15
Simon Russell	33, 36
Soizick Jaffre	31, 104
Steve Reynolds	30, 110
Steven Appleby	7
Tom O'Brien	96
Tracy White	93
Una	51
Victor Szepessy	59
Wallis Eates	112
Woodrow Phoenix	5, 64
Yen Quach	43
Zara Slattery	105
Zoe N. Sugg	45